T0042293

NATIONAL GEOGRAPHIC

In the Tree

Zoe Sharp

Look at me in the tree.

Look at me in the tree.

Look at me in the tree.

Look at me in the tree.

Look at me in the tree.

Look at me in the tree.